# ShePROV

The Monologue Collection, Volume 1

Published by Akilah Logan, 2018.

While every precaution has been taken in the preparation of this book, the publisher assumes no responsibility for errors or omissions, or for damages resulting from the use of the information contained herein.

SHEPROV

**First edition. March 26, 2018.**

ISBN: 978-0-692-10026-4

Copyright © 2018 Akilah Logan

Written by Akilah Logan.

To all of the women who inspired me to write,

**THANK YOU.**

## FOREWORD

So many actors struggle with the idea of working a 9 to 5 to support themselves while pursuing their dreams. "TO BE OR NOT TO BE" an Actor?! That is the question. Here' the answer. If you are truly S.E.R.I.O.U.S about pursuing your dreams then it's importan to support your dreams until your dreams can support you. So, with that said...Create a new way of thinking, create a new way of living, create a new way of being. I always encourage actors to ask three important questions when breaking down their scenes, and strongly believe this applies to real life...to real people, to everyone.

Question #1: What Do I Want?
Question #2: What's Stopping Me From Getting What I Want?
Question #3: Who Am I?

Once you can answer these questions, you will solve your problem but only if you are truly honest with yourself.

Akilah and I met at my One On One Acting Class. We would meet once per week in my New Jersey office in Downtown Newark. Each week we would dive into Scene Work, Character Work and Emotional Work. We would apply my 3 rules to the monologue assigned the week before and each week it would be an eye-opening experience as she discovers the best way to utilize her acting tools. I always end each class with Akilah by saying "do you have any questions regarding our session?" She sometimes hesitates befo she speaks but this one particular night she said she was struggling with moving, making money and being true to herself.

So, I asked her my three favorite questions, "What Do You Really Want? What's Stoppir You From Getting What You Want? and Who Are You?" By the time we finished answering all three questions she was on the path to success.

Here's the deal, we are all given a Special Skill, Talent, A Gift... however you want to word it, whatever "it" is. It's there and here's how you recognize it. It's the first thing you think about when you wake up in the morning. It's the last thing you think about before you go to bed. It's the thing that wakes you up out of your sleep at night. It's your PASSION. And its inside of you waiting to be unleashed. So, let it out and you can turn your dreams into a reality and that salary into a salary.

During our talk, I said to Akilah, "If you have a special skill or a hidden talent. Find a wa to make money doing it. If you think it, Ink it. Create a plan and stick to it."

discovered she's an amazing writer and a good story teller and as you know by now she's written monologue books for aspiring actors and actresses. This will allow her to support her dreams until her dreams can support her. Dream Big.


Wendy Mckenzie
Acting Coach / Creative Director

# SHEPROV: THE MONOLOGUE COLLECTION

## Table of Contents

SHOULD I? ............................................................................. 12

FOR ME ................................................................................. 13

FOOLISH ............................................................................... 18

MIRROR ................................................................................ 20

UNFIT .................................................................................... 22

TRUTH .................................................................................. 28

LOOKING BACK .................................................................. 32

TIME ..................................................................................... 34

KEEP YOU CLOSE .............................................................. 36

LOVE IS A PUNCHING BAG .............................................. 38

COMPLAIN TO ME, ALWAYS ............................................ 40

LET ME OUT ....................................................................... 42

YOU'LL LAND RIGHT ......................................................... 44

REVERSE RIGHT BACK TO ME ....................................... 48

MY BABY .............................................................................. 50

# SHEPROV: THE MONOLOGUE COLLECTION

LOOKING AT ME, LOOKING AT YOU ................................................. 52

ALONE .................................................................................................. 54

FOOLISH TO WHO? ............................................................................ 56

WHAT I REALLY NEED ..................................................................... 57

CHANGE IS GOOD .............................................................................. 60

LIES ....................................................................................................... 62

I LOVE HIM ......................................................................................... 64

BODY ..................................................................................................... 65

CAN YOU BE HONEST? ..................................................................... 68

BRUISED ............................................................................................... 70

LOOK INSIDE ...................................................................................... 73

TOO GOOD? ......................................................................................... 76

CONVINCING ...................................................................................... 77

FREE ...................................................................................................... 80

REMOVED THE BLINDERS .............................................................. 82

JUST BLACK ........................................................................................ 84

100. ........................................................................................................ 87

MIDDLE ................................................................................................ 89

## SHEPROV: THE MONOLOGUE COLLECTION

THE OTHER ............................................................................................. 91

I GOT IT .................................................................................................. 93

PARANOIA ............................................................................................. 96

REAL VS. FAKE .................................................................................... 100

HOUSEWIFE ........................................................................................ 103

GRUDGES ............................................................................................ 105

ULTIMATUM ........................................................................................ 107

EXIT ..................................................................................................... 110

KIDNAPPED ........................................................................................ 112

NO DIFFERENT ................................................................................... 117

OBSESSION ........................................................................................ 120

DECISIONS ......................................................................................... 124

ENTRAPMENT .................................................................................... 126

ACCIDENTS STILL HURT .................................................................. 128

AM I DOWN? ...................................................................................... 129

# SHEPROV: THE MONOLOGUE COLLECTION

# SHEPROV: THE MONOLOGUE COLLECTION

## SHOULD I?

Ok, he said he would be here around 10.
It's 9:45.
He knows that I have something to tell him.
But should I?
As sure as I know my name, he'd kill me if he knew the truth.
Tony, I love you but I've been seeing another-
No, No, No...that's not gonna work.
Hey, so maybe we should have an open relation-
NO...THAT DEFINITELY won't work.
Ok, Nikki. Toughen up. You're gonna have to tell him.
Although, this arrangement gives me exactly what I need.
Tony works all day and all I have to do is cook him dinner and give him sex on Wednesdays. I really don't need to talk to him.
While Jeremy actually talks to me. He's interested in what I have to say!
Who would drop this?
Me! I would!
Come Nikki. He's your husband, not your boyfriend.
Although what point would that make..
It's still cheating.
But I'm not ready to choose.
Then why I am choosing now?!
Because if he finds out NOT by me...he'll kill me.
9:59, oh my God, his car lights.
I'm dead.

**SHEPROV: THE MONOLOGUE COLLECTION**

## FOR ME

I'm doing this for me.
My life choices are not contingent upon your acceptance.
The only thing that matters is…ME.
I'm here, working til' the crack of dawn every day
Forgetting what sleep is just so I can prove to myself that I'm worth
every piece of accomplishment that I achieve.
But you want me to hide so you can feel better.
And for what?
So you can say that you're the man?
The harder I work the more intimidated you get
Why?
Don't you realize that if one eats we ALL eat?
If one wins we ALL win?
We can work together
Grind together
Succeed together
It's not one or the other
We are a partnership
Til' death do us part.
Right?

# SHEPROV: THE MONOLOGUE COLLECTION

## HORROR

When the horrors of my life wore me down I looked to you.
When everything was going haywire and I couldn't find a way, you were able to help me.
When my own mother kicked me out of the house and I had no other place to go,
It was you!
YOU…Helped me.
I have never taken advantage of you!
How can you say that?
I have given you every piece of money that I owed you.
We have no debts.
But now that you see my life is going better and I don't have to ask for help, you have the audacity to think that I turned saddity?
What kind of friend are you?
How could you even think-?
You know, it doesn't matter.
Because now I know.
Now I know what kind of friend you are.
You'd rather have me slumming it up, asking you for scraps
While you're able to play savior.
WELL, NO MORE!
I'm my own person. I finally have the ability to do and help whomever I please.
So, go find yourself another project.
This one…IS OVER.

# SHEPROV: THE MONOLOGUE COLLECTION

## FOOLISH

I was a fool to love you, unconditionally.
I gave you everything...
My love, my life, my soul.
I've made so many reasons...excuses
Why you didn't have to love me back.
You're too busy, you're too tired, you're too stressed.
I loved us for the both of us
But, you're leaving me?
FOR HER?
What did she give you that I didn't?
Did she make life easier for you?
Let you tell her all about the businesses you wanted to do?
Dreamed and imagined all night with you.
Built you up when you couldn't see ANY light of day.
Tell me.
Is she better than me?
I wanna know!
Does she sacrifice the way I do?
Love you the way I do?
Stand by you the way I do?
I didn't think so.
No woman will ever be me.
You'll see. You'll realize it.
But by that time.
I won't care.

# SHEPROV: THE MONOLOGUE COLLECTION

## MIRROR

You know, when I look in the mirror.
I'm checking myself out.
And I'm a pretty good catch.
I'm beautiful
I'm vibrant.
Fun.
So why do I constantly hear you're an amazing woman BUT...
Like there's some list of crouching tiger hidden secret traits that don't I have because apparently there's a BUT.
There's always a BUT.
I'm never enough for whatever reason.
I've heard so many buts that it almost makes me think I am the butt.
I refuse to believe that I have all of these wonderful attributes but according to the men that I meet,
I'm a BUT.
Have you ever considered how that makes me feel?
Have you?
You're telling me that although I'm this AMAZING woman for some reason I don't measure up.
Do you know what that does to a woman?
Do you know how that makes us feel?
Forget us...ME.
I'm such a butt that I've actually compared myself to women on Instagram.
INSTAGRAM!!
Me, a woman that has been so secure in who she is
Is comparing herself to filtered fantasies.
Because of you!
But you don't think about that.
NOPE.

# SHEPROV: THE MONOLOGUE COLLECTION

You act like there's some morse code type of hidden diamond super power that I don't have underneath all this goodness you're pushing away.
But I'm the crazy one.
OK.

**SHEPROV: THE MONOLOGUE COLLECTION**

# SHEPROV: THE MONOLOGUE COLLECTION

# SHEPROV: THE MONOLOGUE COLLECTION

## UNFIT

How are you today?
I'm pretty good, thanks for asking.
Worked all day.
Completed unnecessary deadlines that my boss put on me,
Had my coffee spill all over my blouse that I just bought yesterday,
which is going to be great trying to get out.
Had to eat peanuts for lunch because I forgot my card at home, and my phone died so I couldn't pay online.
Got out of work and ran into 45 minutes of traffic because someone decided to a wheelie on the expressway and everybody just had to look at it.
Get home, the kids were yelling all over the house because the nanny was too busy on the phone with her on again boyfriend.
Sidebar, I think I'm gonna fire her.
Tried to make dinner, but of course you know you were the cook in the house,
So, I burned and not in a good way.
You know what I do best, order takeout.
Finally put the kids to bed and they started asking about you.
Of course tears rolled down my face,
Cause I didn't know what to tell them
I think maybe telling them you went far away won't cut it anymore
What am I supposed to do?
What should I tell them?
How am I going to explain?
Is it fair for their idea of you to be tarnished because of the real you?
Because of what really happened?
How could you leave me with this?
How could you?
You left me!
I can't do this alone.
What were you thinking?
Why did you have to die?
Why can't we go back to that day?
Why can't we get a do over?
I'm all alone, with YOUR children

Their mother is already dead and I am the least qualified person to raise them.
How could you choose me?
Was this some cruel joke?

## SHEPROV: THE MONOLOGUE COLLECTION

## TRUTH

I loved you.
Saw who you were, even when you doubted yourself.
Freely.
I gave time that I wouldn't normally give but for you that's what I did.
And you can't see me?
You can't tell that this is where you belong?
Who am I to you?
REALLY?
TELL ME?! Please!
Because if you can't then why am I here with you, STILL?
I can't go on giving myself to you as if this is where we are but for some reason it's just not clicking for you.
What makes you so blind is that what you're searching for is right in front of your face!
Vulnerable and Open.
Am I not good enough?
Am I not pretty enough?
Am I not sexy enough?
Tell me!
Or am I just the in between you needed to fill the space for someone who's more "fitting"
Is it my voice?
My laugh?
My face?
Tell me.
Because I know you care and I know you love me.
But I'm not fighting a losing battle.
I can't fight for someone that won't admit what is true
Truth, yea.
That's what I'm looking for.

No hold's bar
No strings attached
No hiding behind fear or whatever feels convenient at the time.
Just truth.
Do you think you can do that?

**SHEPROV: THE MONOLOGUE COLLECTION**

# SHEPROV: THE MONOLOGUE COLLECTION

## LOOKING BACK

I'm realizing that I can't love you the way you want me to.
Because I lose myself in you.
Every time I push more love on you,
I disappear.
I know there's other women.
But I don't care.
We have a bond.
A bond that no one else can understand.
Or even see for that matter.
I tried leaving you, thinking I would find myself.
But all I kept doing was thinking about you.
Constantly looking over my shoulder because what I had was easy.
I knew what I was getting into so I didn't have to worry.
Didn't have to take chances.
It was stable. Constant.
It hurts like hell but at least I knew.
I keep wondering if you put someone in my spot or are you thinking about me?
I know there's love and those other chicks don't matter.
I just need to wait until you're ready.
Then I'm sure you'll treat me better.
Right?

**SHEPROV: THE MONOLOGUE COLLECTION**

## TIME

I gave you time.
Maybe more than I should have.
You always had a shoulder to cry on.
Always had someone to lean on.
Our house, never dirty
Never a mess.
Stayed on point.
Played my part.
But that wasn't enough.
Was it?
You needed more, so I gave more
Even when I was empty.
I made something out of nothing and gave it...to you.
Made it look shiny and new so that you wouldn't know that I had to whirl up a can of air...for you.
You mean to tell me, the one time I need you.
I can't find you?
The one time I need you to tell me that I'm beautiful.
Tell me that I'm worth it
You say, I don't need it?
Why am I here?
Are we in this together?
Or have I become your cheerleader and you've become a wall
That's incapable of giving what's received?
But I gave you time and I'm tired.
Now you see me walking out the door and you wanna overload me with love and affection as if it changes things.
It does.
It makes it worse.
All along you had the ability to love,
You just chose not to.

# SHEPROV: THE MONOLOGUE COLLECTION

## KEEP YOU CLOSE

Yo, why do I feel like I'm the only one in this relationship?
I mean, we go out, we have fun, make jokes but
Do you even know me?
Do you even know what I like?
What I don't like?
Do you even know what my favorite color is?
Who am I kidding? I don't know yours.
I just don't think I'm cut out for this.
I got too much going on right now.
You know,
School, basketball, LIFE.
I'm trying to chase dreams and I don't need any distractions.
Especially from you.
But I do like you.
Enough to actually wanna chill.
Talk to while I'm working
But don't get too comfortable, cause I don't know.
I'm not ready.
Commitment is not one of my strong suits.
And I'm not trying to change that.
I have no kids no drama and I wanna keep it that way
So don't go sliding up here...trying to make me love you.

**SHEPROV: THE MONOLOGUE COLLECTION**

## LOVE IS A PUNCHING BAG

So, you're just gonna sit here and act like I don't bother you.
Like whatever I'm doing isn't causing you to cringe every time you see me.
It has to be something because when I come around you,
You change.
What did I do?
One day you're hot, the next day you're cold and you expect me to continue living this way?
Are you kidding me?
What am I?
Your punching bag?
You can say and do whatever the heck you want
Because you think I'm not going anywhere?
Is this how you really want to treat me?
Really?
Someone you claim you love and would die for?!
I know we're on hard times, I know things aren't working like they're supposed to.
Don't take your frustration out on me.
Don't turn me into those other folk that didn't believe in you.
Cause you're losing me!
You said that you would protect me ALWAYS
But who's gonna protect me from you?
Cause THIS ain't a good look.
So, right here, right now we are going to figure this out
Either treat me with the respect I deserve
Or I'm gone.

**SHEPROV: THE MONOLOGUE COLLECTION**

# SHEPROV: THE MONOLOGUE COLLECTION

## COMPLAIN TO ME, always

You know, I sit here and watch you complain about this and complain about that.
But you don't do anything.
You don't work, you don't clean, you're not positive.
And you're low key annoying.
What are you here for?
To torment me?
To get on my nerves?
Remember,
I'm the one that had to hold down the family because your checks weren't coming in and I offered!
You NEVER had to ask, I ALWAYS OFFERED.
And for the life of me I don't understand why you criticize EVERYTHING I DO,
I forgot a couple groceries, I picked the wrong landscaper,
You don't like the TV, the house is too small.
WHAT DO YOU WANT FROM ME?!?!
Maybe it would be better if Johnta helped, you know she was your favorite.
I forgot, she can't.
BECAUSE SHE LEFT YOU, so you stuck with me.
So you can either deal with it or we can part here.

**SHEPROV: THE MONOLOGUE COLLECTION**

# SHEPROV: THE MONOLOGUE COLLECTION

## LET ME OUT

I gotta make a run.
I can't trust who's on my side and who's trying to kill me.
I'm starting to get paranoid because you know I don't trust nobody.
Gotta add security, change locks, send everyone through a new protocol.
It's my time and no one is gonna take this from me.
You think I entered this life to be here forever?
You think I wanna be looking over my shoulder for the rest of my life?
Sleeping with both eyes open?
Constantly thinking someone's out to get me?!
Nah.
I always had an exit plan.
A time limit.
A dollar amount.
I never wanted to stay in too long were I couldn't get out.
I just needed some quick money to get me out of here.
I stayed low, didn't flash no money, kept to myself.
I did EVERYTHING I was supposed
And STILL!
I know someone is after me.
It ain't my fault I'm good at what I do.
It ain't my fault that it takes a woman to build an empire.
I didn't ask for this.
They just came up under me.
And now these fools won't leave.
I'm trying to get out and they keep pulling me back in.
I'm not trying to die
There ain't no 401k
No retirement
No security

**SHEPROV: THE MONOLOGUE COLLECTION**

Just a body bag.
Six feet under.
With everyone saying how much I wasted my life.
But wouldn't dare say it to my face.

**SHEPROV: THE MONOLOGUE COLLECTION**

**SHEPROV: THE MONOLOGUE COLLECTION**

## YOU'LL LAND RIGHT

Look, I don't have time.
Don't ask me about anything.
My life is finally going the way it's supposed to and NOW you wanna talk?
I love you,
Have always loved you.
But I can't rearrange my life every time you get ready to make a commitment.
I have done so much for you that I neglected myself.
DO you know how that feels?
You don't.
You know why?
You never had to.
Everything was always given to you and you never had to work for nothing.
Me on the other hand has had to work for EVERY SINGLE promotion, EVERY SINGLE project and ANY KIND of recognition
So excuse me, if I put you to the side and fight for me.
Don't worry, you'll be just fine.
You'll land on your feet. You always do.

# SHEPROV: THE MONOLOGUE COLLECTION

## REVERSE RIGHT BACK TO ME

Let me tell you something,
I might not be the slim thick woman you want.
But I'm thick. Not fat but thick.
There is a difference.
And the next time you try telling me that I should lose a couple of pounds because you want me to look a certain way,
I'm gonna need to see that 6 pack that you've been working on SINCE LAST YEAR!
Matter of fact, I'm gonna need to see you pick up a dumbbell instead of the remote.
And for the record, I like who I am.
Could I stand to lose a little?
Probably
Am I gonna lose them?
I don't know.
But you will not try to make me feel less of a woman because you can't handle what I got!
AND IT'S NOT EVEN THAT MUCH!

# SHEPROV: THE MONOLOGUE COLLECTION

# SHEPROV: THE MONOLOGUE COLLECTION

## MY BABY

I have been up for 4 hours trying to finish this paper
BUT FOR SOME REASON!
Your needs always come before mine.
Did I ask for this?
Did I ask to be interrupted?
When this has to be done by 9am and I still have to get to work.
Who do you think I am?
Your mother?
It doesn't matter and not my fault that I carried you for 8 months and you decided to be nosey come earlier.
So technically, this work would have been done had you come on the date you were supposed to.
But look at you,
all cute
And bubbly
Innocent
Adorable
Ugh! With a funky diaper.
You're lucky I love you.

# SHEPROV: THE MONOLOGUE COLLECTION

## LOOKING AT ME, LOOKING AT YOU

What is it with you two?
We don't have time for this!
You don't like each other...AGAIN.
I don't know why?
YOU LOOK JUST ALIKE.
Literally, every time you look in the mirror you see your sister.
How is that even possible?
So you can't stand her and the things she says to you
WHO CARES!
You see her every day
This makes no sense.
When are you two gonna patch things up.
This is old and tired
And mom is not gonna be here long.
She needs to see her twin girls getting along.
And not acting like two little dumb savages that
Have no home training.
Get it together.

**SHEPROV: THE MONOLOGUE COLLECTION**

## ALONE

Don't you ever wonder why I go so hard for you?
It's because I know what you can be
Instead of what's easiest for you.
You say, that I only look at your potential and I don't accept you for who you are.
Well, why would I?
The one that doesn't do anything.
Who's ok with being lazy.
Who'd rather sit up here and watch cartoons instead working on music, since you claim that's what you love.
No, I'm not sorry for pushing you.
At least somebody is.
Where's everyone else at?
They were all around when everything was good.
And now look.
Who's still here.
ME....ME!
The one you didn't have time for, the one you overlooked.
When you can't see what's next or who's here standing by you.
Its ME!
I bet you didn't think that huh?
Well, you're wrong.
I didn't change, you did.
You let all those people gas you up, spend your money and now they ain't nowhere to be found.
You need to check yourself and realize who's really there before
You wind up alone.

**SHEPROV: THE MONOLOGUE COLLECTION**

# SHEPROV: THE MONOLOGUE COLLECTION

## FOOLISH TO WHO?

You know, I feel like such a fool.
Why you ask?
Because I sat here and watched you date other women without giving me a piece of a look.
You really had me thinking what the heck was wrong with me?!
I'm beautiful, I'm a ride or die, I love hard.
What?
You mad cause I'm not like everyone else?
Really?
Is that what it is?
Forget that fact the we talk all the time.
Forget the fact that we like the same stuff
And FORGET the fact that YOU LOVE ME!
Nah, that ain't it.
Let me help you out,
You'll never find another person like me.
Even when you find what you think you want.
You'll think of me.
Why?
Because I'm the one you want.
You're just too stupid to recognize it.
You don't even realize how much you love me.
NOW THAT'S HILARIOUS
Who's the first person you talk to?
Me.
Who's the person you call when something happens?
Me.
Who is the person that has been by your side this ENTIRE TIME?
ME!!
Through all of your crazy drama.
And you have A LOT.
But you still have questions?
Hmm, have fun with that.

# SHEPROV: THE MONOLOGUE COLLECTION

## WHAT I REALLY NEED

I can't imagine my life without you.
It doesn't make sense.
You are the air that I breathe
The calm in my air.
What am I supposed to do?
How am I gonna live?
It's like a piece of my soul is being snatched away!
All for the good of you.
Is that what you wanna hear?
Does that make your heart flutter?
Funny how I'm too strong or not vulnerable enough
But you're still here.
Trying to get me to submit.
What more do you want?
When according to my understanding, submission is not forced, it is earned.
What can you offer me but a good lay and bad credit?
You expect me to give you carte blanche over my life when I have yet to see you make an intelligent decision ON YOUR OWN?
You don't get to force me to submit just because you rehearse over and over again that you're the man and the mechanical parts on your body say so.
No, I will not submit to you
However, I can choose to submit to someone who has OUR best interest at heart and in the front of their brain.
So, until you have a legitimate plan for your no, for OUR life.
I can't hear you.

**SHEPROV: THE MONOLOGUE COLLECTION**

## CHANGE IS GOOD

I sit and think about what I did wrong
What I could have done to make this living situation better.
Come to think of it,
I never tried to make you feel like you were less than.
Never made you feel like you were unimportant.
I actually welcomed you with open arms.
Told you that you can do whatever you wanted to.
Stay however long you needed.
Now, you're looking at what I have now like this was easy.
You didn't see when I had to live in a tiny studio apartment in the hood
to pay for my tuition because my parents were too poor to even think
about paying anything.
My dad lost his job and my mom was barely making it.
And let's not forget they already had 2 other kids to take care of.
So, trust me. I worked. HARD. I know where I came from.
And I appreciate it because without that, who knows where I would be.
Hell, who knows if I would be in the position to help you.
So before you go trying to tell me that I changed,
Maybe you should.

## SHEPROV: THE MONOLOGUE COLLECTION

## LIES

So much of my life revolved around you.
Whatever you needed, I was there to help you.
It wasn't because I wanted something from you or felt some sense of duty!
I did it because you were my friend.
Friends do things for each other.
No questions asked!
We have been through too much for us to go out like this.
You're gonna seriously believe this lie over me?!
I'm done Jade.
I'm tired of dealing with these crazy bursts of I don't know if I can trust you.
We are so passed that and if you're still wondering,
Then what am I here for?
Why are we still friends?
Take someone else through this.
We are too old with too long of a friendship for you to diss me.
OVER NOTHING.
A lie someone told you.
When it finally comes to light and you come looking to for me.
DON'T.
I won't be there.

# SHEPROV: THE MONOLOGUE COLLECTION

## I LOVE HIM

I love him.
That's all I know.
I've never been with anyone else like him before.
He had better fashion sense than me, so he told me what to wear.
He didn't want his woman driving so
He drove me wherever I needed to go.
I really didn't go anywhere while he was at work so it really wasn't a big deal.
All I had to do was cook and keep the house clean.
He was so loving and strong...ready to be the man I needed,
And honestly wanted.
I never experienced this before.
That's what we said we wanted, right?
Someone who's a man.
Takes care of everything and I could finally be a woman.
So, if this is what I wanted, why do I feel like I'm in prison?
I told him I wanted to take an art class, so I can start working again.
You know what his first question was?
Not "Oh that's great" or "Where is it?"
But
Who is he?
(PAUSE)
WHO IS HE?!
Really.
My husband of 5 years who monitors everything I do asks me if I'm cheating because I wanted to take a stupid art class.
Why did I even ask?
That's the first and last time I ask him anything.
He turned into someone that I never want to see again.
I know about women who are in abusive relationships.
I don't want that to be us.
He does his job and I do mine.
As long as I stay in my place.
I'm ok.

# SHEPROV: THE MONOLOGUE COLLECTION

## BODY

It's my body, I can do whatever I want.
You just happened to deposit some sperm.
Why should I consult with you in having this baby when you're not the one who's gonna get sick, get fat, go through a slew of emotions and become possibly bedridden.
Your job begins when and IF this baby is born.
We didn't talk about you cheating on me?
Didn't talk when you decided to move to another state ONLY to come back when you saw me with somebody else.
We don't need to have a conversation.
You know what?
I'm gonna have a collective discussion with MYSELF.
Self, do you want to have morning sickness?
NO.
Self, do you want to get fat?
NO.
Self, do you want a baby father who is NOT capable of being a husband?
HECK NO!
And there you have it!
MY DISCUSSION.
You don't like it?
SO WHAT!
This is not a family.
WE are not a family.
You knew who I was when you got with me and you were fine with it.
Don't go asking me to change now because you want me to have this baby and be tied to you forever!
Get out of my **face.**

# SHEPROV: THE MONOLOGUE COLLECTION

## CAN YOU BE HONEST?

Why couldn't you just be honest with me?
I would've went to moon and back for you.
And you know that.
There was nothing that I wouldn't have done for you.
I understand moving away, to start fresh.
I've done it!
But to make such an elaborate lie of who you're living with to keep me close, WHY?
I didn't deserve that.
All I did was love you!
I may not have had as much as I have now,
But whatever I had it was yours!
I HATE YOU!
I hate that I spent so much time trying to make you see who I was when I didn't even know.
But I understand now.
I was your in-between
And you were my love.
How effed up is that?
I was the disposable one.
When the next best train came,
You transferred off and didn't have the balls to tell me.
Now, I'm sitting here with a BROKEN HEART
Trying to pick up the pieces that you left me with.
Thanks.

# SHEPROV: THE MONOLOGUE COLLECTION

## BRUISED

I've been bruised, I've beaten.
Mentally.
I took your words of discord and made them my best friend.
The power of what you said almost caused me to forget who I am.
Internally questioning my being and at times, my existence.
I allowed your fear and your insecurity to latch on to me
Choking the very life of me.
But I stayed.
Stayed because for some reason, I thought you would ACTUALLY see my worth.
Oh, was I wrong.
You balled me up like a dirty piece of lint and threw me in the
Trash as if I tainted your new life.
Broken and Irritated
Not by you, but by me.
Because I saw who you were sooner than expected.
The red flags and gut punches that pierced my soul,
I ignored...because you were comfortable.
Not exciting.
But comfortable.
Until one day, you made the decision that I was supposed to make.
Left me with egg on my face.
So do I hate you?
Or thank you?
Why you say?
Because the essence of who I am is no longer dimmed by your overshadowing banter.
I can finally breathe
Honestly,
I can finally think
Without the constant confusion that wrestled with me.
So again, I've been bruised, I've been beaten.
But I grabbed hold to my self-esteem.
There was no need to ask why me.
Because the level of clarity could have never been achieved
Had you never been brought to me.
So, in fact...thank you.

# SHEPROV: THE MONOLOGUE COLLECTION

For not seeing me.

**SHEPROV: THE MONOLOGUE COLLECTION**

## LOOK INSIDE

Hey,
Tell me what you see.
Tell me what you love about me.
Tell me what you hate about me.
Can you...tell me?
Or don't you know?
Is it because that with every relationship, pieces of you dwindle?
Using non-verbal communication so you won't be deemed...Picky?
Allowing people to dictate who you are
As you stay quiet.
Remaining in silence
As a storm builds within
Because what they claim to see is really a reflection of who they're supposed to be.
So because you don't wanna ruffle feathers and hurt feelings,
You coerce yourself into being the mat
That lies on their back
Being devalued and used.
All because you don't wanna SEEM abused.
But you see.
You know.
That for you to live, this has to be no more.
That for you to thrive, you have to put your feelings to the side
And stand in your truth.
Even if you're the only one standing in the booth.
No one can respect you until you respect you.
No one can love you until you love you.
Block out those who don't know.
If they have to ask,
They'll never know.

# SHEPROV: THE MONOLOGUE COLLECTION

## TOO GOOD?

What do you say to yourself when you realize you've settled?
How can you convince yourself that what you thought you wanted was actually a distraction and a detriment to your ever-changing life?
That the pace you set for yourself has slowed down because someone whispered in your ear?
Not feelings of love and affection
But fear and rejection.
The difficulty in trying to relate has a become an uphill battle
Because the conscious decisions to constantly explain myself has become an everyday chore.
I gave you the keys to drive this relationship
And you crashed it.
Murdered it.
Buried it.
A year away from you helped me to realize that I'm too good for you.
Not the person...the character.
You couldn't handle the basic sense of honesty
So you dragged me along
Singing your same ole song
The sneaky manipulation that ran through your mouth caused some
Unnecessary situations to happen.
But you don't care...do you?
You got what you wanted right?
(PAUSE)
You know, I did to.
I don't realize, I KNOW I'm too good for you.
To differentiate between our levels
It's like trying to figure out who's at the shallow end of the pool
And who's in the deep?
Do we really need to answer that?
I don't give myself a pass or an excuse
For there are none.
Unfortunately for you,
I'm as good as they come.

**SHEPROV: THE MONOLOGUE COLLECTION**

## CONVINCING

I never thought that I would need to convince someone of my compatibility.
Or show more interest than the other
I assumed that we were both adults
Walking through life honestly.
Normally the hard shell that I am,
I cracked open prematurely...for you.
Not because I wanted to...
But you asked.
I walked in constant inner turmoil because your words and actions were never in sync.
Leaving me more confused than I'd rather admit.
Convincing isn't a strong suit of mine.
You're either in or out.
Up or down.
Rarely in between.
But there was something fun about you
Which was the only reason I clinged.
Feelings of unfulfillment turned into
Silence.
And mental stimulation was better alone.
Because I won't convince.
I don't need to convince.
I will never convince.
I don't have the capacity to convince.
The probability of crossing of paths is 0 to none.
But of course, life is joke
Even when you think you've won.
The "maturity level" is nothing but a smoke screen
Of a child that desires to be seen.
Searching for an empty vessel
To fill their need.

# SHEPROV: THE MONOLOGUE COLLECTION

## FREE

How am I considered crazy because I listen to what you say?
Is it my fault that I assumed your word was your bond?
And that you would act your age and not try to con
Me?
The person who wanted you to succeed?
The level of confusion that surrounds your everyday life is apparent as I
reconnect with myself.
The clear and ever-present peace that I have
Was a fleeting notion in your care.
There are many words that could describe how I feel and
What I feel.
I think the best I can come up with is
FREE.
Entangled in your web of neediness
My independence could not permanently coexist.
I looked at myself as if I'm having an outer body experience,
Trying to understand the logic of intentionally
Playing your game.
I can't find anything.
Asking myself am I blind?
Too many questions bombard my brain to which by now I've shut off.
Because there is no point to understanding what I no longer care about.

# SHEPROV: THE MONOLOGUE COLLECTION

# SHEPROV: THE MONOLOGUE COLLECTION

## REMOVED THE BLINDERS

Does my voice scare you?
Or my stature intimidate you?
Since you no longer serve the purpose you thought you'd remain...
FOREVER.
Long gone are the days when I follow behind you
3 steps behind
Hanging on every word
Because I couldn't trust myself to have an opinion.
When I was told being a good wife was being subservient to her husband
with no disagreement.
Strong women were rebellious and
Quiet women were marriage worthy
I was never your helpmate
But an overgrown child that freely
Stayed in her place
But what was the place, actually?
Under your foot where if I wanted anything I had to ask permission?
Or isolated from the world so the only viewpoint I heard or mattered was
yours?
But I have emerged into a woman who loves herself to say
Enough.
The strength that I have right now
Has been buried so deep that I barely recognized myself.
I am not some doormat that needs shaking to keep in line.
Nor am I your private punching bag.
The day my 12 year old daughter came into the bathroom to clean up my
busted lip
Was the day your little woman died.
I've been trying to cover for you so much that living a lie became easier
than standing in truth.
I finally mustered up enough strength to go on without you.
Drop your keys on the counter,
Your belongings are on the porch.
You will not see your children until you get some help.

**SHEPROV: THE MONOLOGUE COLLECTION**

Don't worry, divorce is coming.
Because, if I didn't stop you,
You'd Kill ME.
Officers.

# SHEPROV: THE MONOLOGUE COLLECTION

# SHEPROV: THE MONOLOGUE COLLECTION

## JUST BLACK

Being curious has taken over common sense in ways that I can't even understand.
Constantly, explaining myself for every black person
In chains.
When did I become the postmaster or commentator to discuss why
This man killed this woman or
These girls jumped that girl.
Or why did the little boy steal those sneakers.
News Flash.
I.DON'T.KNOW.
I can only attest to how I was raised.
I can only tell you how my mama slapped the taste out my mouth
When I tried to roll my eyes.
Or how she quickly interrupted my conversation when I was talking to a boy on three way with my friend.
Yea, I was dumb...I know.
But that's all I can tell you.
Stop asking me, why do black people do this or why black people do that?
As if there's some universal cookout that every black person in the world is invited to.
We are different, just as you.
If you don't wanna explain your culture, stop asking me to.

**SHEPROV: THE MONOLOGUE COLLECTION**

# SHEPROV: THE MONOLOGUE COLLECTION

## 100.

Waking up every morning,
Wondering when winter was going to hit and lighten my skin.
I wasn't old enough to actually bleach
But the thought crossed my mind.
Imagining my mom's eyes I quickly declined.
I never understood how the value of beauty was placed on a color that I had no control over.
That my lack of beauty was already decided for me and with no room to discover.
Walking through life for others it must have been easy
"Pretty for a dark skinned girl" always came before the teasing.
Delicate and special were the lighter women
As if my skin tone automatically dubbed me the dingy worker bee.
Too many nights I cried wondering why was this me?
I couldn't be myself much less see my beauty.
Complicated and difficult that's what makeup companies said
So we settled for ashy just to make some bread.
People wonder why it takes so much to uplift a dark-skinned girl,
Ask yourself,
Do you get offended because there's color in your world?
To be put on a pedestal
Or
To carry the pedestal
You can imagine my place.
I was closer to dirt
To be a castaway and hidden.
It took a while to love what I was given
Because I'm constantly bombarded with lighter is winning
Too look in my eyes
Breathe my truth
My skin is bonafide.
100% Proof.

**SHEPROV: THE MONOLOGUE COLLECTION**

## MIDDLE

I constantly have to explain my blackness
Since I'm not dark enough to respect the struggle.
Closer to white is my everyday plight
But they never see me.
I am judged by the non-color of my skin at the same time being criticized for not having enough.
I am the unfortunate middle woman
Having my dark-skinned sisters mad at me because society...NOT ME
Refuses to see your beauty like I see.
You think I don't see your faces when men of all races call me exotic while bringing you to your knees.
For mere acceptance?
You think I don't pay attention to the leave in conditioner and water that I use for a wash n go compared to the 9 products sprinkled with hope and a prayer you need?
I do. I see.
But your anger is not with me.
Just as you have no control over your color,
Neither do I.
I don't think I'm more beautiful,
I am just as beautiful.
We are fortunate to be a part of a long spectrum of color.
I in no way can change a man's heart,
But I can uplift you as you uplift me.
TOGETHER.
Breaking barriers and stereotypes.
TOGETHER.
Our beauty is not based on an ever-changing society.
But in the genuine fact, that we are different.

# SHEPROV: THE MONOLOGUE COLLECTION

# SHEPROV: THE MONOLOGUE COLLECTION

## THE OTHER

I guess I'm not allowed to have a struggle.
Being white and all.
Everything is easy.
Everyone listens to a white woman.
She's so fragile and easily threatened.
Aww poor baby, hold her hand.
How great is that?
Poor little white girl needs everyone's help.
That's real independence.
Last time I checked, I'm not fragile. I'm not easily threatened.
I'm sick of having to put my head down in shame because every time an African American celebrity winds up with a white woman.
I can feel those invisible daggers puncturing my back.
(Ouch)
Trust me.
Our struggles are waaaay different but it's a struggle no less.
My husband's family HATES me.
Would trade me if they could.
Forget we make each other happy.
Forget we have a lot in common.
Forget I own my own business.
Forget that I signed a prenup because his family was well off.
It didn't matter.
I was the white woman that his mama didn't want to see
The white woman they wanted to beg on her knees.
Did I mention they hate me?
And get this?
I CAN COOK!
And I'm not talking unseasoned-No Ma'am.
I make it happen.
But because when I'm in the shower, my hair doesn't thicken up and if I'm in the sun too long I turn into a red pepper.
Everything is my fault.
I'd like to take this time to make a public announcement.
I AM NOT MY ANCESTORS SO PLEASE DO NOT TREAT ME AS SUCH!

**SHEPROV: THE MONOLOGUE COLLECTION**

## SHEPROV: THE MONOLOGUE COLLECTION

## I GOT IT

When I asked you what it would be like?
You told me to trust you because everything was under control.
So, against my better judgment, I said ok.
You got this.
I didn't say anything when we started to get phone calls from bill collectors saying we were 2 months behind.
Large amounts of money leaving our bank accounts for investing in this and investing in that.
I stayed quiet because you said you got this.
What was it you said?
I never trust you with money.
I always go behind you and fix things.
You don't feel like a man.
Tell me.
Do you feel like a man now?
Do you feel accomplished now?
Our savings…GONE.
Our house…GONE.
What we built together…GONE.
When I entered this marriage, we worked together…An equal partnership.
Pushing each other to be the best.
Never have I made you feel insecure.
You did that.
Never have I changed the way I act with you.
You're not good with money.
Deal with it.
You're artistic, I'm not.
I'm a corny bookworm, you're not.
There is absolutely no way that I could do what you do!
Your talent…incredible!
Who said you needed to do and be everything?
If that's true, what am I here for?
Where the other lacks, the other fills in.
That has always been our motto.
But you took it upon yourself to dabble in something that you hate doing and it cost us everything.

Now, you tell me what would've happened, if I didn't clean up this mess?
Cause YOU know...
I GOT US.

# SHEPROV: THE MONOLOGUE COLLECTION

# SHEPROV: THE MONOLOGUE COLLECTION

## PARANOIA

How am I doing?
You wanna know how I'm doing?
I haven't been outside in weeks.
I have 7 different locks on my door and I sleep with my lights on.
And that's IF I can sleep.
Waking up in the middle of the night because what I think is someone trying to break into my home are trees banging from the wind.
I don't order take out or have friends over.
I keep my curtains closed with an alarm system for my windows.
I stay safe.
That's how I'm doing
I'm safe.
My mom comes over once a week to bring me groceries and keeps me company.
She's the only one I can deal with right now because I don't trust none of you.
I live my life within these walls.
I protect myself within these walls.
I can't even let fresh air and light in my own apartment because when I walk to the window,
I can still see his face!
The man that we were hanging out with having a good time.
The man you all called friend.
The man according to you was a good guy.
Who broke my window
Dragged me from the couch to the floor and
Ripped off my clothes
As I'm trying to use every bit of power that I had to fight him off.
Feeling his slaps and punches because for some reason I didn't like what he was doing!
My face so bloody and beat down that I couldn't recognize myself.
Violated, Alone, and Confused.
Ready to die.
All because I told him no.
And you wanna ask me how I'm doing.

# SHEPROV: THE MONOLOGUE COLLECTION

# SHEPROV: THE MONOLOGUE COLLECTION

## REAL VS. FAKE

I woke up one morning, I knew something was wrong.
I called my husband at work, he told me to schedule a doctor's appointment and rest for the day.
I listened.
Fell asleep on the couch and woke up with sharp pains in my stomach.
I called my husband and told him I was going to the hospital because something wasn't right.
He was there when the doctor told me that it had to be indigestion or heart burn
because everything looked fine.
Not soon as I reached the exit,
I dropped to my knees and I saw blood running down my leg.
They rushed me into an emergency room and I had my baby.
But she wasn't breathing.
No one could tell me what happened!
I wasn't given an explanation.
Just an I'm so sorry.
You're sorry.
This child that I grew to love for 5 months slipped before my eyes.
Without a trace.
Right before my eyes.
I was happy…proud.
I thought finally…it's my turn.
I've waited 5 years to get pregnant.
Through scheduled sex, lots of sex.
Counselling.
Fertility treatments.
My body has been through so much these past years that it's hard to believe that I got pregnant.
Let's not forget that I'm definitely not in the "younger" pool of women.
But it happened.
I did everything I was supposed to and still no child.
I didn't even want children but my husband did.

I sacrificed for our family and I grew to love and want the child for myself.
Crazy, right?
I somehow can't get the idea out of my mind that I killed my baby.
Maybe she knew deep down I didn't want her.
But I loved her.
Was my love fake?

# SHEPROV: THE MONOLOGUE COLLECTION

## HOUSEWIFE

I have sat here and waited for someone to tell me what's going on.
With blood stains still on my shirt.
And dried up tears.
No one has given me any information, they just send me home.
I come here EVERY.SINGLE.DAY.
Just wanting answers.
The person that murdered my husband and daughter is still alive.
And you think, that I'm gonna sit here and do nothing?
I know I don't have police training.
I don't know what combat training is.
But you know what I am?
A housewife.
Which means I have organized for the best of them.
Found things in places you would not believe.
And I have alllllll the time that you seem to not have to find their killer.
I will use every waking moment to seek justice for my family.
I won't burden you with this any longer
Just stay out of my way.
This is my one and only.
One and done.
Go ahead and underestimate me.
I dare you.

**SHEPROV: THE MONOLOGUE COLLECTION**

## GRUDGES

When was the last time you called your mother?
I know you guys don't have the greatest relationship but it's not about that right now.
It doesn't matter what she did or didn't do for you when you were growing up.
She's fighting for her life.
She doesn't have that much time.
Oh, she didn't tell you?
The cancer came back…accelerated.
They're giving her 4 months.
You're sitting up here holding grudges and attitudes when the woman that brought you into this world, may die…TOMORROW.
But that's okay for you huh?
Because the scars of growing up were oh so deep you just can't bear to forgive.
Is that what you want your daughter to see?
Her mother not being able to forgive.
You're not the stellar parent you think you are…and please believe she's gonna have some problems with you too.
You're not exempt.
So busy trying not to be her when you're turning into her.
We all know mom was bitter, mean and nasty…to EVERYONE.
You think if you're not careful that's not gonna be you?

# SHEPROV: THE MONOLOGUE COLLECTION

## ULTIMATUM

This pain in my chest causes me to forget the arguments we had.
It reminds me that none of that matters anymore.
Claiming who was right and blaming who was wrong
Seems so trivial.
When I can't even sit up straight without grasping for air.
And I always need help.
Doing everything on my own has caused me to rely on people.
For basic movements.
So many times I ignored my doctors.
Take it easy, Mera.
Slow down Mera.
You're doing too much, Mera.
Adding to the unnecessary pressure of being a superwoman
Coupled with #teamnosleep
I am now bedridden.
My body has literally shut down on me.
And every movement I try to make it feels like shards of glass piercing my skin.
So I don't care…anymore.
I can't play the part of running your life as I ruin mine.
We're supposed to be partners not enemies.
Building empires not tearing them down.
We both need to do equal work.
Cause I can't carry this company by myself.
I'm tired.

**SHEPROV: THE MONOLOGUE COLLECTION**

# SHEPROV: THE MONOLOGUE COLLECTION

## EXIT

I have tried my hardest to forget you.
Deleted your social media.
Tore up your pictures
Burned your clothes.
Moved to a new apartment.
5 years…5 years.
You were my life, my love,
You were my soulmate, I thought.
But you lied to me.
Told me you needed time
You needed SPACE.
When in all actuality, you were planning your exit.
What you didn't account for is me finding out BEFORE
You left.
If men like you put more time into relationships and being honest,
There would be less crazy in the world.
And y'all wonder why women turn loco!
Because you are too much of punk to tell me it wasn't working.
Making decisions on your own that affected the both of us.
SHUT UP!
You thought I wasn't gonna check your phone.
I did.
You thought you were being followed.
That was me.
Made fake profile pages to catch you.
Yup. Right over here.
And see, the problem is what you're gonna say is "Oh my girl's crazy!"
But you conveniently forget what drove me to this.
I gave up 5 years for you.
Built a home, a life!
And you were just gonna slip on out the back door!

**SHEPROV: THE MONOLOGUE COLLECTION**

Tell me why I should take this knife and slit your throat.
No need to lie…Here's the evidence right here.
Go ahead and LIE!
Huh? I can't hear you.
You're scared?
You should be.

**SHEPROV: THE MONOLOGUE COLLECTION**

## KIDNAPPED

Look,
Last thing I remember,
I was walking,
A van pulls up
Two men jumped me
Stuffed my face with a white cloth
And now I'm here...in front of you.
I don't know who you are or why I'm here.
I'm just a computer analyst.
So unless you wanna fill in those blanks.
We have nothing to talk about.
Hello? Hello?
Do you hear me talking to you?
You're just gonna sit there and stare at me.
With nothing to say, no answer?
Look, this has to be some sort of mistake.
You've got the wrong person, I won't say anything just let me leave.
What's your name? huh?
Excuse me…Don't walk away from me!
Where am I?
I don't know what kind of game you're playing or who you're looking for but whoever it is,
I'm not them!
Hello? Hello?
Answer me!
Please!
Somebody help me!
What do you want from me!
Where am I?

# SHEPROV: THE MONOLOGUE COLLECTION

# SHEPROV: THE MONOLOGUE COLLECTION

## CAN'T MIND MY BUSINESS

You wanted me.
You got me.
Waited 2 years to plan the perfect mission.
There was no way anyone would've figure it out.
I mean, you're an intelligent girl.
However, inexperienced. Careless.
And NOT very detailed.
It's clear you had help,
I doubt you would've made it this far alone.
All you had to do was go to work, mind your business, make your little rounds and leave.
But you couldn't just leave it alone, could you?
You just had to open the envelope.
Just had to look
You think I'm gonna let my hard work go down the drain?
And let THEM WIN?
I gave them 17 years.
17 years!
And they decide to fire me without a cause.
Which means no pension, no security. NOTHING.
I came to work. Kept my head down. Stayed out of trouble.
But that wasn't enough for them.
They wanted someone younger, less experienced.
No responsibilities so they could pay them less.
I'm supposed to just find my way.
FIND MY WAY!
How??
Yea, I'm gonna find a way.
I'm gonna take what's mine.
What's owed to me.
I'm gonna drain them so dry they won't know what hit em.
I'm warning you,
Stay out of my way.

# SHEPROV: THE MONOLOGUE COLLECTION

# SHEPROV: THE MONOLOGUE COLLECTION

## NO DIFFERENT

What is the world coming to?
When will this end?
It's not enough that we are black in this neighborhood.
I have to make sure my family is safe. IN THIS NEIGHBORHOOD.
We don't bother anyone.
None of you tried to get to know us.
You assumed we came from a ghetto area and decided to ostracize us.
But did I let it bother me? No.
Did I treat you any different. No.
So please.
Tell me what I'm supposed to tell my 7 year old daughter when she asks where is her older brother?
What am I gonna tell her?
I have complained and complained to each and every one of you sitting up there.
Telling you that my son was being mistreated.
Telling you he was being bullied by the same kids you claimed he was friends with.
And what did you say?
It's just kids being kids and laughed it off.
Is it kids being kids now?
That boy shot my son because he wouldn't give him his sneakers!
I don't care if you're sorry.
I don't want your condolences.
There is nothing you can say that will bring my boy back.
What if that was your son?
Would you have let it go as far?
Or would you have called the cops on my son?
Would it still be kids being kids if it was the other way around?
You can see me and my family as a threat but I can't see you the same way?
You don't think I hear you joking about the new black family that doesn't act like normal black people, whatever that means.
When will you look at me as an equal?
We put our clothes on the same way you do, eat the same food you do.
And this is how you treat us?
I send my kid to school here every day praying that he comes home safe.

From school?!
That's what I pray.
I had to worry about my son walking while black because you!
None of you know what that's like.
Then I had to look you people in the eye because you allowed their son to bully my son and now he's dead.
I don't wanna hear your speeches, I don't want any of your hugs or sad faces.
What I wanna know
What are you gonna do about it?

**SHEPROV: THE MONOLOGUE COLLECTION**

# SHEPROV: THE MONOLOGUE COLLECTION

## OBSESSION

I was blinded by hatred.
Or whatever I thought it was.
I searched for you day in and day out.
There's nothing more than I wanted then to see your ugly face behind bars.
But come to think out it,
You don't deserve jail.
You don't deserve the luxury of breathing.
You don't deserve to live
You don't get to serve a sentence when you didn't give those women a choice.
No.
Not while I'm still alive.
How many women Travis?!
How many women have you lied to?
How many women have you murdered?
They fell for your lies.
Fell for your charm
Wanted someone to love them and what did you do?!
You killed them for what?
Sport?
You are a sick maniacal psycho.
I should kill you right now.
Not so tough, are you?
I would be doing those women an injustice if I let you live.
I would be doing myself an injustice!
What? Huh?
You've never met me?
You don't remember me?
Good.
The only face I want you to think about is the one that got away.

# SHEPROV: THE MONOLOGUE COLLECTION

## DECISIONS

You think they're gonna look after us?
What gave you that idea?
Just because they gave you a place for 6 months 4 years ago,
You think you owe them your life?
Don't trust them.
You don't need them.
They only want the reward money.
They don't love you.
I'm the only one that cares about you.
Who will keep you safe.
Did your mom even look for you after you left?
No.
She just took the money you gave her and went on her way.
When are you going to realize she will never be the mother you need?
She doesn't have it in her.
It's always been about what she wanted.
Nothing has changed.
And the more you keep feeding her addiction.
Feeding her money.
She's not going to change.
She's gonna get us caught.
Is that what you want?
If we're gonna do this, you have to let her go.
We don't need the dead weight.

**SHEPROV: THE MONOLOGUE COLLECTION**

# SHEPROV: THE MONOLOGUE COLLECTION

## ENTRAPMENT

You knew all along.
You sat here and told me there were no more secrets
No more lies.
You can't imagine how my life has been.
I've been trying to figure out who I am and where I come from.
Who were my parents?
You knew.
EVERYTHING.
Year after year.
Dead end after dead end.
It never ceased to amaze me how my trail always got cold.
I kept asking myself why?
Why was it so hard for me to figure out who my parents were?
Then it came to me.
YOU.
It all points to you.
Who were you protecting me from?
The man I first met or the man you really are.
You expected me to go through my life and not find out who you really are.
Now because of you,
I have to decide whether to love you and keep this secret
Or call the Feds.
Was this your plan from the beginning?
To trap me into loving you?

# SHEPROV: THE MONOLOGUE COLLECTION

## ACCIDENTS STILL HURT

To the love of my life
My best friend
The one who never told me I talked too much.
The one who laughed when I tried to cook because I burned everything
The one I loved unconditionally.
Life without you has been colorless.
And quiet.
I get sick to my stomach realizing I will never see you again.
Still in denial, pacing the floor.
I keep going to our favorite places hoping that I'll see you.
Wishing you were some sort of spy agent person
And you're secretly looking out for me behind the shadows.
But I know it's not true.
We were pretty simple.
Crunch berries in the morning
Comics were our midnight tease
As we listened to Pat Benatar.
Well, I made you listen to Pat…Benatar.
But our life was good.
Ya know.
We were planning for kids but that didn't happen.
There's so many things we planned for.
But could never do.
As much as I know this was an accident.
It's hard for me to forgive much less move on.
Knowing there's no penalty.
Nothing.
Because of an accident.
They took you away from me.
And I get to live with your memory
While their lives aren't changed.
I love you.
Miss you.
Still need you.

# SHEPROV: THE MONOLOGUE COLLECTION

# SHEPROV: THE MONOLOGUE COLLECTION

## AM I DOWN?

The only thing that concerns me is to make sure that I catch whatever Rat that hits my desk.
For the past month, I have planned and schemed because I knew you were innocent.
I worked like crazy every single day
Putting my life on the line
Risking everything to collect evidence to prove your innocence,
And you have the nerve to ask me if I'm all in?
Why?
Because it's not happening as quickly as you like?!
No, Be quiet.
I don't wanna hear it.
You've had your time.
I'm talking.
Do you even know WHAT I'm risking?
Forget my career that I worked so hard for.
But every time I walk into the DOD's office,
Pulling up files that haven't been touched in 5 years gets logged in MY name.
Cameras…everywhere monitoring each office I walk in scanning MY face.
Oh, and let's not forget the bio metrics passwords that I -not you have to use for those great top secret restricted areas.
So what am I doing?
I'm committing about 60 crimes while trying to prove you are innocent of one.
Any questions?

# SHEPROV: THE MONOLOGUE COLLECTION

The only person that can block the precious cargo that desires to burst...is
**YOU.**

# SHEPROV: THE MONOLOGUE COLLECTION